A Hen in a Fox's Den

by Donald Rasmussen and Lynn Goldberg

BASIC READING

BERKELEY·CALIFORNIA

To Parents and Teachers

Donald Rasmussen and Lynn Goldberg developed the BASIC READING SERIES (BRS) in the early 1960s at the Miquon School, a small parent-teacher cooperative near Philadelphia. At that time, most children were taught to read using the "sight" or "look-say" method epitomized by the "Dick and Jane" readers, and many were left behind. Don and Lynn knew there must be a better way, so they spent five years developing their own reading program based on the work of the renowned linguist Leonard Bloomfield. They called their method *"inductive whole-word phonics, with a strong linguistics research base."*

After tryouts in inner-city and suburban schools around the country and almost a dozen revisions, the BASIC READING SERIES was published by Science Research Associates (SRA) and enjoyed great success. Over the years, other reading methods have come and then gone out of favor. Now, decades later, phonics is recognized as the scientific approach to reading instruction, and the BASIC READING SERIES is once again available.

Whole-Word Phonics Simplifies Learning

Where BRS differs from traditional phonics practice is in the methods by which it reaches the same goal. Traditional phonics practice will typically ask children to "sound out" single letters first ("*b* says *buh*") and then "blend" individual letter sounds into whole words ("*buh-ih-tuh* says *bit*").

The authors found it more effective and realistic to start children off with whole words (meaningful *combinations* of letters) and let them discover how individual letter-changes affect word pronunciation. In this way, children always see letters in their true perspective as parts of a whole, interacting with the other parts. They learn how the letter *b* functions *in a particular situation* instead of "what the letter *b* says."

Moreover, an unnecessary intermediate step is avoided. Why have children translate the letters *b-i-t* into a false language first (*buh-ih-tuh*) and then *re*translate that into the word *bit*? Experience shows that most children can go directly from the letters *b-i-t* to the word *bit* without the extra step.

Email all inquiries to:
Peter Rasmussen, Editor
info@BasicReading.com

Website: BasicReading.com
ISBN 978-1-937547-12-7

Inductive Method Enhances Discovery

BRS introduces the child first to words like *man, ran, fan,* and *pan,* using them in sentences, drills, and exercises that provide many opportunities for observation and discovery. The child sees that the *-an* sound and spelling are constant in these words while the introductory consonant varies. Next introduced are a series of *-ad* words: *sad, mad, had, pad,* and so on. The child begins to see that certain initial consonants have the same effect here as they had in the *-an* words. Now an early inductive conclusion becomes possible: confronted with the letters *p-a-d,* the child discovers that it starts like *pan* and ends like *mad.* Therefore, it must be *pad.* The child has figured out a word independently!

Thus, starting with the simplest and progressing to more complex patterns, the program gradually accumulates more and more word patterns from which children can draw reliable generalizations of their own about the connections between spellings and sounds. It gives the children plentiful opportunities to develop confidence and automatic responses to each pattern and to apply their generalizations to new words.

Controlled Vocabulary Builds Confidence

The reading vocabulary of BRS is closely controlled according to spelling patterns. These patterns are revealed to the learner one by one so that the language that confronts the student at each stage is regular, consistent, and predictable. Fortunately, English spelling *does* contain a core of consistent patterns for representing most sounds, despite the apparent inconsistencies. Linguistic science has helped to classify these, and classroom trial and error enabled the authors to sequence them for maximally efficient learning. The controlled release of vocabulary, organized by spelling patterns, ensures that children will encounter the unusual and nonconforming patterns only when they are ready for them — after they feel secure with the regular and reliable features of the language, and after they have read a large body of complete stories, thus building a background of confidence and solid achievement.

What's Covered in Level B?

BRS is divided into Levels A to F, with a reader and a workbook for each level. In Level B, children are introduced to three new vowel sound-spelling relationships: *e* as in *pet, o* as in *pot,* and *u* as in *cut.* The new words introduced follow the same pattern as the words in Level A: 3-letter words in which a vowel appears between two consonants. In addition, children meet initial *g* and *y,* final *x,* and six new sight words.

Contents

a	i	e	o	u
bat	bit	bet	cot	but
cat	hit	get	Dot	cut
hat	kit	jet	got	hut
mat	lit	let	hot	jut
Nat	pit	met	jot	nut
pat	sit	net	lot	rut
rat		pet	not	
sat		set	pot	
		wet	rot	
		yet		

Pit-a-Pit-Pat

Pit-a-pit-pat!

Pit-a-pit-pat!

I am a cat

and I can bat.

Pit-a-pit-pit!

Pit-a-pit-pit!

I had a fit—

I cannot hit.

Pit-a-pit-pet!

Pit-a-pit-pet!

I got set

to hit it yet!

Pit-a-pit-pot!

Pit-a-pit-pot!

A cat cannot

hit a lot!

Kim Gets a Wig

Kim got a hat.

But the hat did not fit Kim.

It was big and Kim was sad.

Pam was Kim's pal.

Pam said to Kim,

   "Get a pin.

   Get a pin and pin it."

Kim said, "But I cannot get a pin.

   I cannot pin the hat."

Pat was Kim's pal.

Pat said to Kim,

   "Get the hat wet.

   It fits if it is wet."

And Kim said,

   "But I cannot wet the hat."

Sal was Kim's pal.

Sal said to Kim,

   "Get rid of the hat, Kim.

   It's a man's hat.

   Get rid of the hat and

   get a cap."

"Not a cap," said Pam and Pat.

   "Get rid of the hat and

   get a wig."

And Kim got a wig!

Pam's Fan

It was hot in Pam's hut.

Pam said to Nan,

   "I am hot.

   I am hot and I cannot nap."

Nan said to Pam,

   "If it is hot, Pam,

   get a fan.

   Set the fan in the hut."

And Pam said,

   "O.K., Nan. Dad has a fan.

   I can get Dad's fan."

And Pam ran to get it.

Pam set the fan in the hut

   and got into a cot.

The fan ran and ran.

And Pam had a nap.

Rags and Jet

Dot and Kim had pets.

Rags was a pet of Kim and Dot.

And Jet was a pet—a pet cat.

Rags was mad at Jet.

If Rags ran to Dot, Jet ran to Dot.

If Rags ran to Kim, Jet ran to Kim.

If Rags sat in Dot's lap, Jet had
to sit in Dot's lap.

Rags got mad and said,

"I am mad at Jet.

If I sit in Kim's lap, Jet has
to sit in Kim's lap.

If I sit in Dot's lap, Jet has to
   sit in Dot's lap."
But Dot said to Rags,
   "Jet is not a big pet.
   Jet cannot get a hat.
   Get Kim a hat, Rags."
Rags ran and got Kim a hat.
Kim had to pet Rags.
And Rags said,
   "I am big, and I can get hats.
   But Jet cannot.
   I am not mad at Jet."

I Got . . .

I got a fat bat—
   not a fat cat,
      not a fat rat.
I got a fat bat
   to sit in a hat!

I met a wet pig—
   not a wet wig,
      not a wet fig.
I met a wet pig
   and got it to jig!

I got a hot pot—
   not a hot dot,
      not a hot cot.
I got a hot pot,
   and I fan it a lot!

a	i	e	o	u
bag	big	beg	dog	bug
lag	dig	leg	fog	dug
rag	fig	peg	hog	hug
tag	jig		jog	jug
wag	pig		log	lug
	wig			rug
				tug

Tim

Tim ran to the log.

Tim sat.

A pig ran to the log.

The pig sat.

Did the log tip?

The log did tip!

Did Tim sit?

Tim did NOT sit!

Sad Tim!

A-Rig-a-Jig-Jog

A-rig-a-jig-jog!
  A-pit-a-pit-pat!
A big fat hog
  met a fat tan cat.

A-pit-a-pit-pat!
  A-rig-a-jig-jog!
The hog and the cat
  did a jig at a log.

A-rig-a-jig-jog!
  A-pit-a-pit-pat!
A fog hit the log,
  and the hog and cat sat!

The Nut in the Net

Peg the pig ran to a pit.

It was a big pit.

A nut was in it.

"I can get into the pit," said Peg.

   "And I can get the nut."

But a net was in the pit.

"I can get the nut," said Peg.

Peg ran to get the nut.

Peg bit the nut.

But Peg's leg got into the net.

Wag the dog ran to the pit.

Wag was Peg's pal.

"Wag! Wag!" Peg said.

   "I am a sad pig."

Wag said to Peg,

"Get to the rim of the pit."

"I cannot," said Peg.

"I had to get a nut in the pit.

But I got into the net."

"Tug," said Wag.

"I did tug," said Peg.

Wag got into the pit.

Wag bit the net.

"I can rip the net," said Wag.

Wag bit and bit and bit.

The net began to rip!

"I did it! I did it!" said Wag.

Wag ran to dig.

And Peg did a jig.

Let's Jig, Jig, Jig

Let's jig, jig, jig!
  Let's jog, jog, jog!
Let's tag, tag, tag
  a log, log, log!

Let's tag, tag, tag
  a log, log, log.
Let's jig, jig, jig
  in a fog, fog, fog!

Let's pet, pet, pet
a hog, hog, hog.
And the hog can jig
in the fog, fog, fog!

Let's jig, jig, jig!
Let's jog, jog, jog!
Let's get, get, get
a big hot dog!

a	i	e	o	u
Dan	bin	Ben	Don	bun
fan	fin	den	on	fun
man	pin	hen		gun
pan	tin	Ken		run
ran	in	men		sun
tan		pen		
an		ten		

| by |
| my |
| why |

Don sat <u>by</u> Ken in the sun.

"Ben is <u>my</u> pet dog," said Don.

   "Ben is <u>my</u> pal."

"<u>Why</u> is Ben a pal?" said Ken.

"Ben gets <u>my</u> cap," said Don.

Don sat <u>by</u> his dad and said,

"<u>Why</u> is it fun to sit in the sun?

   <u>Why</u> is it fun to sit <u>by</u> <u>my</u> dad?

   <u>Why</u> is it fun to get wet in a fog?

   <u>Why</u> is it fun if it's bad?"

The Mad Pig

In a van is a pig.
  On the pig is a wig.
On the wig is a hat.
  In the hat is a pin.

The pin jabs the hat.
  The pin jabs the wig.
The pin jabs the pig.
  Bim! Bam! Bim!

The pig is sad.
  The pig is mad.
The pig ran.
  The pig hid.
The pig did
  a rig-a-jig-jig!

Ten Pigs and a Hen

Ten pigs sat in a pigpen.

A fat hen ran by.

"The pigpen is big," said the hen.

  "I cannot run in my pen."

"Why?" said the pigs.

"My pen is not big," said the hen.

The hen ran into the pigpen.

The hen said, "Pigs! Pigs!

  Can I run in the pen?"

A pig said, "My pen is a pigpen.

  It is not a hen pen!"

But the hen began to beg.

"Pigs! Pigs!" said the hen.

"It is fun to run in a pigpen.

It is not fun to run in a hen pen.

Can I run in the pigpen?"

The pigs let the hen run in the pen.

The hen said,

"I can run in the pigpen!"

But the ten pigs sat in the pigpen.

"Pigs! Pigs!" the fat hen said.

"It is fun to run. Run, pigs, run!"

The hen and the pigs ran in the pen.

The fat hen began to dig.

The ten pigs sat.

"Pigs! Pigs!" said the fat hen.

"It is fun to dig.

Dig, pigs, dig!"

The hen and the pigs dug in the pen.

The fat hen sat in the pigs' pan.

The fat hen got wet.

"Pigs! Pigs!" said the fat hen.

"It is fun to sit in a big pan.

It is fun to get wet.

Get into the pan, pigs.

Get wet, pigs! Get wet!"

The pigs got into the pan.

The hen and the pigs got wet.

The ten pigs said,

"A hen in a pigpen is a pet."

The fat hen said,

"A pig in a pigpen is a pal."

The hen and the pigs did a jig.

The ten pigs had a pet.

The hen had ten pals.

Meg's Pet Pig

Meg had a pet pig.

The pig had a pen.

But the pig did not sit in its pen,

and it did not run in the pen.

The pig sat and sat on a log.

It did not get into its pen.

Meg began to tug at the pig, but
   the pig did not get into its pen.

Meg was sad.

It was not fun to tug and tug.

Meg met Ben and Ken in a van.

The men began to tug at the
pig, but the pig did not run.
"Tug, Meg," said Ben and Ken.
Meg and the men began to tug.
But the pig did not get in its pen.
The pig sat on a log.

Ziz-ziz-ziz!

A bug sat on the pig's leg!

The bug bit the pig's leg!

Bim! Bam! Bim! Bam!

The pig began to run.

The pig ran into its pen!

The Hot Sun

"It's fun to dig in the sun,"
  Dot said.
  "I can dig a pit."
Dot sat and began to dig.
"The sun is hot," Dot said.
  "But it is fun to dig."
Dot dug a big pit.
But the hot sun hit Dot.

"I am hot," said Dot.

Dot sat on a log and said,

   "The sun is hot and I cannot dig."

Dot began to nap on the log.

The sun hit Dot.

And Dot got a bad suntan.

Dot said, "If I dig, I am hot.

If I nap on a log, I am hot.

It's not fun to get a bad suntan."

Dot was sad.

Dot said,

"The sun cannot get into my pit."

Dot got into the big pit.

And the sun did NOT hit Dot.

Dot had a nap in the pit.

And Dot did not get hot.

Ten Hens

Ten hens ran in the sun.

   Ten hens had lots of fun.

The hens did not hug.

   The hens did not tug.

The hens did not sit.

   The hens did not hit.

But the hens did run,

   In the pen, in the sun.

a	i	e	o	u
bad	bid	bed	nod	bud
lad	lid	fed	pod	mud
mad	rid	led	rod	
pad		Ned		
		red		
		Ted		

a	i	e	o	u
cap	hip	pep	hop	cup
map	tip		mop	pup
tap			pop	up
			top	

Ted's Pup

TED: Bud is my pup and Bud
can sit up and beg.

DAD: O.K., Ted.
Get Bud to sit up and beg.

TED: Bud! Sit up!

(Bud sits up and begs.)

37

TED: Bud can get on top of his hut!

DAD: O.K. Let Bud get up on top.

TED: Bud! Get on top of the hut!

(Bud gets on top of the hut.)

DAD: Can Bud get my hat?

TED: Run and get Dad's hat, Bud!

(Bud runs and gets Dad's hat.)

DAD: And can the pup get in bed?

TED: Dad! Dad!

My pup cannot get in bed!

DAD: And why not?

TED: My pup cannot get in bed!

Not if I am not in bed!

BUD: Yip! Yip! Yip!

The Sad Pup

Peg had a pet pup.

The pup was sad.

Not a bit of ham was in its pan!

The pup had to get fed, but

  Peg was in bed.

The pup ran to Peg's bed.

The pup began to tug at Peg's
   bed, but Peg did not get up.
The pup had to get fed.
The pup got up onto the bed.
The pup began to nip at Peg's leg.
Peg sat up and said,
   "Bad pup! I cannot nap."

But the pup sat up to beg.

It began to beg to get fed.

"My pup is not bad," said Peg.

"It did not get fed."

Peg got up and got the pup's pan.

Peg got ham and cut it into bits.

"The ham is in the pan," Peg said.

The pup ran to get the ham.

But the pup ran into the pan.

The ham was on the rug, and
   the pup was sad.

But Peg was not mad.

"My, my, my!" said Peg.

   "I can get it up."

Peg got the ham into the pan.

   Peg set the pan by the pup.

Peg's pup WAS fed.

A Hop and a Pop

Hop! Hop! Hop!
   A bug sat on a bud.
Pop! Pop! Pop!
   The bug sat in the mud.

In the Fog

Pegleg, the piglet, had a nap.

Pegleg got up and said,

"I can run in the fog!

It's fun to run in the fog!"

But Pegleg's dad, Hogleg, said,

"A pig cannot run in the fog.

The fog is wet.

Sit in the pen, Pegleg."

"But it is fun to run in the fog,"
   said Pegleg.
And Pegleg ran into the fog.
"The fog is wet," said Pegleg.
   "But I can run and hop in it."
Pegleg ran on and on in the wet fog.

Pegleg ran into a big pit of mud.

Pegleg sat in the mud.

"The mud is wet," said Pegleg.

Pegleg was sad and said,

"My dad said not to run in the fog.

The mud is up to the top of my legs.

The pit is big.

I cannot get to the top of it."

The sad, wet piglet sat in the pit.

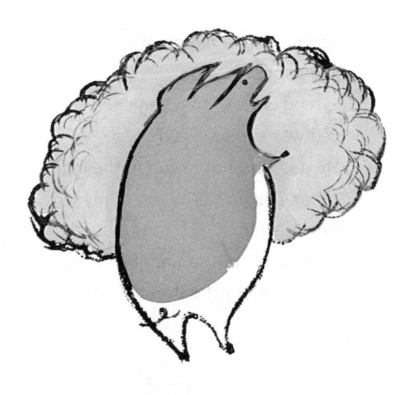

Hogleg was sad and said,
  "My piglet is in the fog.
  My piglet cannot get to its pen."
Hogleg ran into the fog.
Hogleg ran on and on.

Hogleg ran into the big pit of mud.

Hogleg had to lug Pegleg to the
  top of the pit.

Hogleg led Pegleg to the pigpen.

And Pegleg had fun in the pigpen.

A Bug and a Pig

A bug sat on a fat pig,

sat on a fat pig,

sat on a fat pig.

On top of the pig,

the bug did a jig,

the bug did a jig,

the bug did a jig.

Said the bug to the pig,
"I can hop, I can jig,
I can sit, I can dig,
on top of a pig,
on top of a pig,
on top of a pig!"

Said the pig to the bug,
"I can hop, I can hug,
I can sit, I can tug,
and hit at a bug,
and hit at a bug,
and hit at a bug!"

The bug did NOT sit
on top of the pig,
on top of the pig,
on top of the pig.

The PIG sat on top of the bug!

_a_	_i_	_e_	_o_	_u_
gas		yes		bus
				Gus
				us

_a_	_i_	_e_	_o_	_u_
ham	him	hem	mom	gum
Sam	Tim		Tom	hum
tam				sum

_a_	_i_	_e_	_o_	_u_
cab	bib	web	Bob	cub
jab	rib		cob	rub
tab			job	tub
			rob	
			sob	

no

go

so

"Go to bed, Sam," said Mom.

"No! No! No!" said Sam.

   "I cannot go to bed yet."

"Why not?" said Mom.

"The sun is up," said Sam.

   "And it is hot.

   So I cannot go to bed."

Let's

A cat met a pup.

The pup met a pig.

The pup said, "Pig!

Let's hum and jig!"

The pig met a hen.

The hen met a cub.

The hen said, "Cub!

Let's sit in a tub!"

The cub met a hog.

   The hog met a rat.

The hog said, "Rat!

   Let's nap on a mat!"

The rat met a man.

   The man met a dog.

The man said, "Dog!

   Let's run and jog!"

The Red Bug and the Cobweb

A tan bug sat by his cobweb.

"If lots of bugs get in my web,"

   said the tan bug,

   "I can get fed."

A red bug ran up to the web.

The tan bug said,

   "Red Bug! Red Bug!

   Get into my web."

But the red bug did not get into it.

The tan bug said,

　"Get in, Red Bug!

　It is fun in a cobweb."

But the red bug did not get in.

The tan bug said,

　"A bug can nap in a cobweb."

Hop! Hop! Hop!

Red Bug began to hop in.

"Yes! Get in!" said the tan bug.

　"It's fun in a web."

Red Bug did not get in the web.

Red Bug BIT at the web.

"No! No!" said the tan bug.

The tan bug ran to get Red Bug.

But Red Bug ran and hid in the mud.

The tan bug did not get Red Bug.

And so the tan bug was not fed!

A-Rub-a-Dub-Dub

A-rub-a-dub-dub!
  Ten pigs in a tub!
A-rig-a-dig-dig!
  Ten pigs did a jig!

A-rum-a-dum-dum!
  Ten pigs can hum!
A-rop-a-dop-dop!
  Ten pigs can hop!

A Cat on a Bus

Tom had a job.

Tom had to get to his job on a bus.

Tom's pet cat, Rob, sat by him.

A red bus ran up to Tom and Rob.

A big man ran the bus.

The bus man said to Tom,

   "Men can get on my bus.

   But cats cannot get on."

So Tom said to Rob, "No, Rob.

Cats cannot get on the bus.

Go and sit on the rug and nap."

But Rob began to rub Tom's legs.

"No, no, Rob!" said Tom.

Tom got on the big red bus.

But Rob did not go to nap.

Rob ran by the bus!

Ten men got on the bus.

And so did Rob!

Rob ran up to Tom.

"No! No!" said Tom.

But Rob got onto Tom's lap.

Tom had a bag in his lap.

Tom said,

"Get into the bag, Rob."

And Tom hid Rob in his bag.

But Rob did not sit in the bag.

Rip! Rip! Rip!

Rob began to rip the bag.

Pop! Pop! Pop!

Rob was not in Tom's bag!

Rob ran zigzag in the bus!

"No! No!" said Tom.

   "Cats cannot run in the bus."

Rob ran up to the bus man.

Rob got into his lap.

And the bus ran into the mud!

The bus did not go.

"My job is to run the bus,"
said the bus man.
"If a cat sits on my lap,
I cannot run the bus.
If the bus cannot go,
Tom cannot get to his job.
Rob is a bad cat.
If Tom lets his cat get on my bus,
Tom cannot get on!"

"I did not let Rob get on the bus,"

Tom said.

"The ten men let Rob get on the bus.

But I can get the bus to go.

And the men can get the bus to go."

It was a job!

But the bus began to go.

So the bus man was not mad.

"If Rob sits on Tom's lap,

Rob can sit on the bus,"

the bus man said.

So Rob did not run.

Rob sat and let Tom pet him!

A Wet Cub

Dot dug a pit in the wet mud.

Bob, Dot's pal, ran up.

"Can I dig in the pit?"

   Bob said to Dot.

"Yes," said Dot. "It is fun.

   Sit and dig."

Pit-pat! Pit-pat! Pit-pat!

"A cub! A cub!" said Dot and Bob.

The cub began to tug on Bob's leg.

Dot got upset.

The cub began to hug Bob.

"Get up and run, Bob," said Dot.

Bob said, "The cub is not bad.

   Let the cub sit and dig, Dot."

Bob and Dot began to dig.

But the cub ran into the pit.

It sat in the mud.

It was in mud up to its hips.

"No! No! Bad cub!" said Dot.

But the cub did not get up.

"I can get it," said Bob.

And Bob got into the pit.

But the cub did not get up.

The cub began to hug Bob.

"No, cub!" said Bob.

Bob began to tug at the cub's leg.

"I cannot get it up," Bob said.

"Get up, Bob," said Dot.

"If I get it mad, I can get it up."

Dot began to dig.

Dot let the mud hit the cub.

The cub got mad!

The cub ran up to the top.

"Let's go! Let's run!" said Dot.

"A cub is fun, but not if it's mad."

a	i	e	o	u
Max	fix		box	
wax	mix		fox	
ax	six		ox	

oh

"<u>Oh</u>, me! <u>Oh</u>, my!
   A dog bit my cat!
<u>Oh</u>, me! <u>Oh</u>, my!
   A hog bit the dog!
"<u>Oh</u>, me! <u>Oh</u>, my!
   A log hit the hog!
Sad cat, sad dog, sad hog.

Max Is Six

"I am six! I am six!

So I am big," said Max.

"Mom said if I am six,

I can get a pet dog."

Max ran to his mom and said,

"I am six and I am big.

Can I get a pet dog?"

"Not yet, Max," said Mom.

"Why not?" said Max.

"Run into the den," said Mom.

"Into the den? Why?" said Max.

"Can I get the dog?"

But Mom said, "No, go into the den."

Max was sad.

But Max DID go to the den.

A big box was on the rug!

The box was as big as Max.

A red tag was on the box.

The red tag said, "TO MAX."

"It's MY box!" said Max.

Max began to tug at the lid.

Pop! Pop! Pop!

The lid was up.

"Oh-oh-oh-oh!" said Max.

"It's a dog—a pet dog.

It's a dog I can hug and pet!"

Max ran to his mom and said,

"I got a pet dog.

I am six, and I am big."

The Big Box

AL: My pal Tom has a big box.

It's a big, big, BIG box.

It's as big as a box can get!

SAL: Why is Tom's box so big?

AL: It has a pin in it.

SAL: A pin? But a pin is not big.

Why so big a box to fit a pin?

AL: The pin is in a wig.

        And the WIG is in the box.

SAL: Oh. But a wig is not so big.

        Why is the box so big?

AL: The wig is on a man.

SAL: And the MAN is in the box?

        O.K. It IS a big box—

            but not big, big, BIG!

AL: But the man is on a bed.

        And the BED is in the box!

SAL: O.K. It is a big, big box.

        But it's not big, big, BIG!

AL: Oh, yes it is.

        The bed is in a hut.

        And the HUT is in the box.

SAL: Yes, Al, it IS a big, big, BIG box!
But it's not as big as a
box can get.

AL: Oh, yes it is.
The hut is in the sun!

SAL: The hut is in the sun?
And the SUN is in the box?

AL: Yes, the sun is in the box.

SAL: Oh, it IS a big, big, BIG box!
It's as big as a box can get!
And it's a big, big, BIG fib, AI.
It's as big as a fib can get!

A Hen in a Fox's Den

A fat hen sat on a log in the sun.

Red Fox ran up to the log.

Red Fox met the hen and said,

   "Fat Hen, let's go to my den."

Red Fox led the fat hen to his den.

The fat hen ran into the den.

A big hot pot was in the den.

Red Fox said to the hen,

   "Fat Hen! Fat Hen!

   Hop into the pot!

   Hop into the pot!"

But the fat hen did not hop in the pot.

The hen got up on the fox's bed.

Red Fox said,

"Fat Hen! Fat Hen!

Hop into the pot!

Hop into the pot!

It is fun to sit in a pot!"

But the fat hen did not get in.

The fat hen sat and sat.

Red Fox got upset.

Red Fox ran to the hen and said,

"Fat Hen! Fat Hen!

Hop into the pot!

Hop into the pot!

It is fun to sit in a pot!

It is fun to get wet in a pot!"

But the fat hen did not get in.

The fat hen said to the fox,

"I cannot get in the pot, Red Fox.

But I can run and get a pig.

The pig can sit in the pot.

A pig is fat!

A hen is not fat!

A pig can get in the pot!"

Red Fox said, "Yes, yes!

Get a pig.

Get a fat pig to sit in the pot!

Run and get the pig!"

The fat hen got up and ran and

ran and ran and ran.

Red Fox sat in his den.

Red Fox sat and sat and sat.

If I Mix . . .

If I mix
   a lot of cobs
      in a box of webs,
         can I get
            a box of cobwebs?

If I mix
   a lot of hums
      in a box of bugs,
         can I get
            a box of humbugs?

Pattern Pages

Pattern Page

1

(page 1)

_a_	_i_	_e_	_o_	_u_
bat	bit	bet	cot	but
cat	hit	get	Dot	cut
hat	kit	jet	got	hut
mat	lit	let	hot	jut
Nat	pit	met	jot	nut
pat	sit	net	lot	rut
rat		pet	not	
sat		set	pot	
		wet	rot	
		yet		

Pattern Page

2
(page 11)

_a_	_i_	_e_	_o_	_u_
bag	big	beg	dog	bug
lag	dig	leg	fog	dug
rag	fig	peg	hog	hug
tag	jig		jog	jug
wag	pig		log	lug
	wig			rug
				tug

Pattern Page

3

(pages 20-21)

_a_	_i_	_e_	_o_	_u_
Dan	bin	Ben	Don	bun
fan	fin	den	on	fun
man	pin	hen		gun
pan	tin	Ken		run
ran	in	men		sun
tan		pen		
an		ten		

by
my
why

Pattern Page

4

(page 36)

_a_	_i_	_e_	_o_	_u_
bad	bid	bed	nod	bud
lad	lid	fed	pod	mud
mad	rid	led	rod	
pad		Ned		
		red		
		Ted		

cap	hip	pep	hop	cup
map	tip		mop	pup
tap			pop	up
			top	

Pattern Page

5

(pages 52-53)

no
go
so

_a_	_i_	_e_	_o_	_u_
gas		yes		bus
				Gus
				us

_a_	_i_	_e_	_o_	_u_
ham	him	hem	mom	gum
Sam	Tim		Tom	hum
tam				sum

_a_	_i_	_e_	_o_	_u_
cab	bib	web	Bob	cub
jab	rib		cob	rub
tab			job	tub
			rob	
			sob	

Pattern Page

6

(page 73)

oh

__a__	__i__	__e__	__o__	__u__
Max	fix		box	
wax	mix		fox	
ax	six		ox	

Made in the USA
Monee, IL
12 February 2025

12077472R10057